# SUMMARY

If you are currently a business owner or you're considering becoming one that intends to use Vending and Craft events as an option to increase sales and exposure, THIS is the book to read! Ms E is sharing her knowledge and expertise based on being in business for over 12 years, having gone to events in and outside of the city of Cleveland, while building relationships in the process, so that you will yield results without it costing you the hefty price of "trial & error" on your own.

This guide will give you practical information on How To:

* Determine what type of events are best for your product or service and how to find them.

* How to receive better engagement from customers as they walk by your table.

* Create the simple table display to draw more customers to you.

This guide is meant to be read, to take notes and to be referenced as often as needed to assist you in your journey of sales and results when you set up your table at an event.

When you find yourself having questions or in need of

more guidance in this process, Ms E's website and social media platforms allow you to connect to her to setup up appointments. She knows what it's like to feel lonely on this entrepreneurial faith journey. Now you have a link that understands and will assist you in this process.

# ARE YOU SURE THAT YOU ARE READY?

## A GUIDE FOR VENDORS

## MS E

Copyright © 2019 J Merrill Publishing, Inc.

All rights reserved. No part of this publication may be reproduced, distributed, or transmitted in any form or by any means, including photocopying, recording, or other electronic or mechanical methods, without the prior written permission of the publisher, except in the case of brief quotations embodied in critical reviews and certain other noncommercial uses permitted by copyright law. For permission requests, write to the publisher, addressed "Attention: Permissions Coordinator," at the address below.

ISBN: 978-1-950719-20-4 (Paperback)

ISBN: 978-1-950719-22-8 (eBook)

Any references to historical events, real people, or real places are used fictitiously. Names, characters, and places are products of the author's imagination.

**FIRST** printing edition 2019.

J Merrill Publishing, Inc.

434 Hillpine Drive

Columbus, OH 43207

www.JMerrillPublishingInc.com

## CONTENTS

| | |
|---|---|
| *Who Is Ms E and Why This Book Is For You* | vii |
| 1. Stay Ready & You Won't Have to Get Ready! | 1 |
| 2. Small, Big Cleveland | 3 |
| 3. Transitioning / Balancing Full Time | 5 |
| 4. Using Your Smartphone Wisely And Keep Your Apps Up To Date | 9 |
| 5. Keeping It Professional | 11 |
| 6. Finding & Accepting Events | 15 |
| 7. Taking Your Business On The Road | 19 |
| 8. Confirm Your Budget And Match Your Audience | 23 |
| 9. Clear Everything - Make No Assumptions | 25 |
| 10. Advertising For Events | 27 |
| 11. Event Checklist | 29 |
| 12. Event Day: Showing up & Setting up - ON TIME, EVERY TIME | 33 |
| 13. Inside vs Outside Events | 35 |
| 14. Returning Calls and Making Connections | 41 |
| 15. Get YOUR Money! | 43 |
| *Notes* | 49 |
| *Acknowledgments* | 53 |

## WHO IS MS E AND WHY THIS BOOK IS FOR YOU

Hey there!

I'm Ms E, The Author of Are You Sure that You Are Ready?~A Single's Guide to Preparing for Marriage; the Baker behind Ms E's Glory Loaves, and the Organizer of Ms E's Home Re-Organization.

I started my first business, Ms E's Home Re-Organization where I clean and organize homes and offices, relieving your stress one room/project at a time, in April 2007; Ms E's Glory Loaves, which is cinnamon raisin bread made in different sizes and various fruit options; in September 2008, published my book in June 2011, my workbook in April 2016 and completed my certifications as a Relationship Coach by August 2012 while working full-time at an Accounting Firm since May 2002. In January 2012 during a 21-day Fast with my church, I asked "Where should I go from here?" I sensed that God was moving, and I wanted guidance to go for another job. God instructed me to focus on my businesses full-time. Now, please note that before 2007, the thought of being an entrepreneur was the furthest thing from my mind, so when God began directing me to start these businesses, I had NO IDEA of where they would lead me. Instruction to write my first book came after I was simply organizing a bunch of notes I had in several memo pads. It took me 5 years to finally complete it because I was trying to talk myself out of having to do it, mostly because the notes were meant to encourage "me" during my singleness. Later, reader testimonials revealed that not only was I not alone but also that I am an encourager for others. I was encouraged by a close friend that writing one book was only the beginning, which I did not believe to be necessarily true. Here we are 8 years, 2 books and 1 workbook later, WHO KNEW?? I will admit this time around, after receiving the instruction to complete this book, I complied much quicker. Being disobedient comes with consequences, obedience comes with rewards.

I've answered many questions over the last few years on the topic of vending. I've observed a LOT of things that could be better, realizing that I would've appreciated some assistance getting started, yet didn't have a reference. It's my desire to see us ALL succeed and if by being obedient to my purpose helps another to be successful, then I'm doing my part. As an Organizer, my attention to details wherever I am, is not something I ignore or overlook. The suggestions I give have yielded an increase in sales after making the adjustments to tables. Being a part of the panel for The Art of Vending, an event held here in Cleveland back in May 2019, confirmed that there is a need for a source and resource for vending information. Well, here we are!!

My goal with this resource is to provide you with the knowledge and tools for you to be successful in your future vending experiences.

Having a business does not always mean that you have to be a vendor at an event. The type of business you have and knowing your target audience, (your market, your typical consumer), is the biggest obstacle to overcome in business. Your product or service will NOT be for everyone, so your goal is to focus on being accessible to your ideal customer.

**Suggestions for Products and Services at Events:**

**Fashion Shows/ Music Performances / Plays**

Accessories

Clothing

Bath & Beauty Products

Select Food and Dessert items

**Craft/Vendor Shows**

Books

Unique Gift and Household Items

Art & Handmade Items

Select Food and Dessert items

**Health Fairs**

Bath & Beauty Products

Personal Trainers & Instructors

Financial Services

Health / Wellness Authors & Coaches

Healthy Food and Dessert items

If you know of at least 3-5 people that truly enjoy your products to be in attendance AND you've been invited by the event host/coordinator, this is "usually" a good recipe for success.

## 1. STAY READY & YOU WON'T HAVE TO GET READY!

I heard this statement years ago and adapted it as one of my mantras, especially as it relates to business. As an entrepreneur, one of the main keys to your success will be to stay prepared. You should not be without business cards, whether physical or digital and a clear Elevator Pitch so that you can concisely convey your message. Inventory is necessary for most businesses, whether it's office supplies, cleaning, cooking, baking supplies, etc. Do your best to stay on top of these items so that you will not be unprepared. When you order items that need to be shipped, give yourself enough lead time so that you'll have your items in hand AND on time. You may think, I can just purchase it from the store. This may be a day you're running around town looking for an item that is limited in number or just may be discontinued and you do not have a backup plan. Prepare and plan to avoid these situations as much as possible.

1. Make the list

2. Check your budget

3. Schedule your shopping trip and location(s)

4. Get It Done - request assistance, when needed

Though you may not currently be in a position to purchase "everything" you need right way, keep track of the items you will need over time. Pace yourself and plan your budget so that you can add accordingly, as funds and needs increase.

Another mantra I use is: You Have Not, because You Ask Not & If You Don't Ask, the Answer will Always Be No. You never know when an opportunity will come your way, yet you should be prepared to receive it.

## 2. SMALL, BIG CLEVELAND

One of the main things I've learned, especially within the last 7 years is that as "Big" as the city of Cleveland is, it's just as "Small." You never know who knows whom, that knows YOU. As you attend various events and functions you will meet a LOT of people and people WILL talk. What will they say about you? What have you said about them? When sharing a story, usually a funny one, with someone new, I've always made it a point to leave out names and keep things light. If I have an issue with something or someone I've come across, and I need to vent about it, I save that for my close inner circle because I KNOW that's where it will stay. Sharing negatively amongst the general public could backfire on you and create a situation that may hinder your growth and progress for your business.

## 3. TRANSITIONING / BALANCING FULL TIME

Whether you're working a full or part-time job, adding an additional stream of income lasts by creating balance. Learn to be a good steward of your time and your energy. When you're serious about being successful, you may find yourself getting distracted and even overwhelmed at times. Connect with business owners like yourself. You need a safe environment to vent and receive encouragement, especially during challenging times. When you need to slow down, or even step away to refresh yourself, take the time to do it. You are more productive when you can truly focus on getting things accomplished vs just staying "busy."

If leaving your "9-5" is your plan, take your time and Count the Costs. Many entrepreneurs step out too soon and unprepared, then find themselves struggling and needing to go back. Even if you do all that you know to plan your "out," setbacks will occur. It is a part of the journey. Do your part and allow God to do His, just be sure to stay sensitive to His guidance and instructions, especially when it comes to leaving steady employment. Pray and ask for several confirmations. Do the research, take the classes, even investing in a mentor will prove beneficial when doing it BEFORE stepping out full-time.

When you have a spouse, children and even your friends and family, make time to spend with them. You would prefer them to be with you during your journey versus losing them because of your journey. Teamwork makes the dream work, so get your team together so that you will have time to spend with them. Here are a few suggestions:

1. Plan and prepare your meals instead of regularly eating out – healthier eating habits will keep you healthier for your business AND family.

2. Ask for HELP! Assign chores and tasks to your family; Hire an intern, virtual or live assistant for your business needs. Be aware of your limits and limitations.

3. Create a Daily To-Do List to ensure tasks for the day get completed.

4. Make time for yourself to shut down, at least for a few hours each week. Your brain and your body needs rest and time to recoup from the stress from the week. Exercise, meditation, massages are forms of self-care that aid in relieving stress.

5. Extended vacations may not occur often in the beginning, so plan a weekend getaway to a hotel outside of the city, (check Groupon, Hotwire, etc. for deals and specials) at least once a year. Relaxing does not have to

cost a fortune. You can "ball on a budget" when you plan and save.

The necessity to do these things is even greater when you have a mate. Your relationship, especially a marriage, should be as much of a priority as your business. Prayer and communication are key components in a successful relationship. The support and encouragement of your mate goes a long way and will take you even further than doing it alone.

## 4. USING YOUR SMARTPHONE WISELY AND KEEP YOUR APPS UP TO DATE

Your phone puts practically everything at your fingertips now. Get the training you need so your phone is the "asset" it is designed to be. For the money that is invested in "gadgets" they are now a business expense because they are designed to allow you to work more efficiently and effectively. Your calendar should be your "first" go-to when planning meetings and especially booking events. This will minimize stress and avoid double-booking. All personal and business appointments, events, deadlines and meetings can be scheduled on your calendar with reminders and locations. You can "invite" people, add notes and set up repeating events. Keeping track of these things and paying attention to the notifications will keep you on track and organized, which will lead to greater success.

Notes, Notes & More Notes!! There are several different apps that will allow you to take notes and keep them handy for future reference. As you have thoughts throughout the day, instead of relying solely on your memory, voice record or jot down the note so that you can refer to it later. Since distractions cannot always be avoided, recording or writing your thoughts down, will minimize the chance of you forgetting. The Notes can also keep a Checklist of the items that you will need to have on hand for your events and even for the supplies you need to prepare for the events.

Reminder: Your phone and its apps are ALWAYS updating. If you do not have your settings on "Auto Update," Check your Goggle Play Store or iTunes App Store regularly to ensure that the apps you use, especially those used for your business are Up to Date. These updates ensure that everything is working like it should with the other apps that are linked to them. (Ex: if you update Instagram without updating Facebook, you will encounter issues when you try to post to both at the same time.) Make it a practice to check either before going to bed or in the morning after your regular routine before starting your day.

## 5. KEEPING IT PROFESSIONAL

As a business owner, your level of professionalism is ALWAYS being watched: in the streets, when you're speaking with anyone, (in person, on the phone, online, emails & text messages). Some customers will intentionally attempt to provoke you and even challenge your prices. Rise above their attempts with grace and professionalism. Your goal should be to leave a positive and lasting impression, which leads to repeat business and referrals.

What you wear is important! You should look like you planned to attend the event. First impressions make lasting impressions. Even when the event is casual, YOU ARE A BUSINESS and the face of YOUR business, represent it well. Consider the event and the venue, (casual, semi-formal, formal), and represent accordingly. Your attire and appearance matter as much, possibly even more than, your table set-up. Your hair should be neat, clothes should be neat, clean, ironed and representative of your brand as much as possible. When you look as if you just rolled out of bed and ran to the event, it leaves a questionable note to your customers, (Yes, this happens). If you've questioned or critiqued restaurants that appeared "unclean," believe that those walking by your table may feel the same way.

Keep your table space Neat, Clear and Welcoming. This is a TABLE, (usually 6', 8' or 9'), not a store front. A Vending Event is a "sampling" of the items you have available. Give your customers an experience they will remember so they will want to contact and purchase from you again in the future. A creative, yet clean table is a welcome table. Having your table cluttered with items is overwhelming for potential customers to even approach. The area around and underneath your table should be clear as well, for your own safety. The shopping experience at an event is meant to be quick & simple. What you are selling should be very clear as soon as you approach the table. If you have too many items that are NOT connected to your brand, the average person will move past your table.

PUT DOWN YOUR PHONE! Your phone should NOT appear to be more important than your customers. When customer traffic is slower at an event, yes that's a good time to do a quick post on social media to remind your customers and followers in the area to stop by to support the event. However, if a potential customer is walking by, put the phone down until after you've engaged with the customer. Always be aware of your surroundings and customers. Smile and Speak to people as they are walking by. Some people try to walk by without looking, but a nice smile and pleasant "Good morning" or "Good afternoon" will turn their heads in your direction, potentially leading to more conversation AND a sale! No engagement = No sale.

Unless your children are attentively sitting at your table and can articulate your product or services, they REALLY should be left with a sitter. They will be a distraction. You are running a business at an event therefore you are representing YOUR business, ALWAYS.

It is a beautiful thing when your mate is supportive of your business and attends events with you. Let's keep the P.D.A. (public displays of affection), to a minimum. Again, you are representing your business at an event, treat it as such. Anyone sitting at your table represents YOUR business, and should be working equally diligent in assisting with making sales, not just sitting or standing in your face, or rubbing all over you.

Conversations, rather with other vendors or the person you brought to assist you, should be at a minimum. If you're in the middle of a conversation, push pause when a potential customer approaches your table, after all, that is the main reason you are there. When you see another vendor distracted when a customer approaches, let them know as well.

The same applies with food. Plan and eat your meals before or after the event. If you need to snack on something, keep it simple so that you can interact easily with your customers. How would you feel when approaching a business to purchase a product and the representative is more concerned with their sandwich than conducting business with you? This would be YOU at an event.

Stay close to your table as much as possible. When you want to shop with the other vendors, arriving early allows more time for this. This can be made easier when you bring someone to join you at your table, so your table is always attended to. I've found that most vendors have been nice enough to "watch" your table if you need to step away for a few moments, just be considerate and mindful of your time away, they have customers as well.

## 6. FINDING & ACCEPTING EVENTS

One of the frequently asked questions has been: How do you find out about and get invited to events? My answer - There are several ways:

Social Media provides several options for finding events:

**1.** Groups - I belong to several groups on Facebook that regularly post about events ALL Year long. The key is to read through them, inquire on pricing, read through their contracts and follow the directions for completing their process. Group suggestions: check categories for your city, product and services.

**2.** Advertisements (either Sponsored/Paid ads or via Posts to pages, both business and personal) Many people will post about having or being a part of an event. When you see the words: Vendors Wanted, Vendors On Site, or Vendors Will Be Available to Shop With; These are your opportunities to inquire via call, inbox or email. Usually, the post has instructions on how to submit inquiries.

PLEASE READ ALL THE DETAILS before reaching out. Most of the time the answers are right in front of you.

3. Hashtags, especially on Instagram - for Example: #ClevelandVendors #VendorsWanted #LocalEvents #ClevelandEvents #ShopLocal; Typically, event planners will use these Hashtags within their posts to be found. You should also include similar Hashtags on your posts: #ClevelandVendor #ShopSmall #ClevelandBusiness #SupportLocalBusiness so that you can be found as well. Though "Cleveland" is referenced here, replace it with your city or city of interest.

4. Referrals - when your friends and family know you're interested in being a vendor because you've posted in the past, they will send you information or tag you in a post. Look into it after thanking the sender. This is also their way of showing their support for your business.

5. Check your Direct Messages (DM's), Inboxes and Emails - many event coordinators and planners will reach out to you because of your Hashtags and/or your product if they feel that it will be a good fit for their event. An event that you've attended in the past will reach back out to you for future events. Remember YOU KNOW your product and the best audience and market for it. You do not have to accept every invitation, but you can read through the details, check your availability and budget to see if it appears to be a good match. Be sure to respond in a timely manner, whether it's a Yes or Thank you for considering me, but I have a previous event scheduled. Please keep me posted about future events, (a polite No).

Create a system for keeping track of the events that you are invited to and those you accept. I created an **Event Opportunity Form** for each of my businesses and put them in my **Upcoming Event folder**, which I review at least once a week while I'm planning the upcoming week's tasks. I separate those that are PAID, PENDING and even the DECLINED to ensure that I've responded to them. Once you have agreed to and paid for the event, add it to your calendar so that you minimize "double-booking" for that same day and time. Double-booking can create issues for some coordinators if you need to leave their event earlier than the event ends. If you have 2 events on the same day, communicate with the coordinators of both events as soon as possible. This keeps things professional, you in good standing and most of them will work with you. When there are contracts involved, print out a copy for your records and keep it with your Sales and Inventory Tally Sheets. (Hopefully, you have already read through the terms of the contract BEFORE submitting payment and the printed copy serves as a reminder on or before the event.)

## 7. TAKING YOUR BUSINESS ON THE ROAD

There are MANY opportunities and potential customers and clients that are outside of the city, county and state limits where you reside, GO GET THEM!! Depending on your business, you can take your product or service on the road to other venues, in other states. Allow the road to be your friend! When you have more of a unique product or service, this can be more profitable than if you we a part of a Direct Sales company since those are usually booked on a "first come, first serve" bases, which tend to go quickly.

It's good to be able to travel with a friend or spouse, especially when going somewhere new, however allow yourself to grow and to be open to the adventure. Take the necessary precautions for your safety and embrace the chance to connect with new vendors and customers, which also extends your market reach and SALES!

I hadn't considered traveling outside of the Northeast Ohio area with my loaves until I spoke with a vendor who mentioned it during our conversation. She spoke about taking her products on the road because she knew there was more outside of Cleveland. I inquired as to how she found out about these opportunities and of course she mentioned Social Media. She told me about an event she was attending in Detroit, Michigan and shared the contact information. I reached out, paid the fee and saved the date. Originally, we spoke about carpooling together, but as the event date approached, she informed me that she had mistakenly double-booked and wouldn't be going to MI with me. Though it was my first event in MI, it was NOT my first solo road trip plus I enjoy the peace of the road. Though I did not make a lot in sales "that day," I connected with some great and supportive women that invited me to future events they were having and a couple of them came up a couple of weeks later to one of my Coffee & Conversation events. Each trip to MI resulted in additional sales and new connections and friendships.

## Event Opportunity Form

How I found out about event:
- ☐ Invite from Coordinator _____ ☐ FaceBook
- ☐ Previous Event Attendance _____ ☐ Instagram
- ☐ Referral: _____ ☐ _____

Venue: _____
          Address/City/State             Venue

Purpose/Theme of Event: _____

Donation Item requested? ☐ Yes: _____ ☐ No

Date(s): _____ Time: _____

Table Fee: _____ Fee Due Date: _____

Event Contact: _____ Phone: _____

Email: _____

Contract Received: ☐ Yes     ☐ No     ☐ N/A

Method of Payment: ☐ PayPal: _____
☐ Cash App: _____
☐ Money Order: Payee & Mailing address _____

8. **CONFIRM YOUR BUDGET AND MATCH YOUR AUDIENCE**

You will have many opportunities come your way as the word spreads about you and your products, which is great. Every event may NOT be for YOU. You should be selective where you and your products show up. As you attend different events, keep a **Sale and Inventory Tally Sheet** - this helps you calculate sales from each event. At the end of each month, as you review your numbers, compare what is working and where adjustments can be made. If it's an event that repeats regularly, (quarterly, annually), you can review the numbers, note the items that sold well and prepare accordingly.

Example: If an event is offering vendor tables for $125 - here's a minimum of what you should consider:

1. Is this my target audience? If you've been there before, your Tally Sheets will answer this for you. If you've made improvements to your products and/or display materials, your sales would be reflective

**2.** Calculate how much product will be needed to make AT LEAST $125 plus gas money

**3.** How long is the event? 3 hours, 5 hours or longer (2 or 3 days) and is it enough time to earn your table fee AND a profit?

**4.** Do you need to bring your own table, chair or will they be provided?

**5.** What time does the event start? How early can you arrive to setup?

**6.** Where is the event? Local or Out of Town

**7.** Is it an inside or outside event? Check weather conditions

**8.** How will you get to the event - Drive or Fly?

**9.** Will you need to book a hotel to stay overnight or will you be able to come back home that same evening?

**10.** If driving, are there highway tolls involved & how much are they round-trip?

**11.** What will you receive for this event cost? Some offer ad placement in programs and on flyers used to market the event; some include a meal or refreshments; others may include advertisement AND refreshments.

9. **CLEAR EVERYTHING - MAKE NO ASSUMPTIONS**

As you attend more events, you will learn more and more of the different styles and intentions of those coordinating an event. Create a list of questions, even a checklist, of the items that matter most to you for you to have a successful return from attending an event. There should be certain "Must Haves" for you. Assumptions breed disappointment. When contracts are given, READ THROUGH THE ENTIRE CONTRACT. The contract is meant to cover the basics for what will be provided and the requests to be met by you. When a contract is not provided, usually for smaller events, ask ALL the questions you need BEFORE paying. Usually, this minimizes the need to request a refund or the hassles that accompany that process. Release yourself from the pressure of needing to accept any and all invitations that are sent to you, just be sure to respond to them. A polite "No" is simply stating "Thank you for the invite, unfortunately, I have a prior engagement scheduled for that day, but please keep me in mind for future events." Know and understand how and where your product or service fits into an event along with your reason for attending.

## 10. ADVERTISING FOR EVENTS

When you sign up as a vendor to attend an event, it is JUST as much YOUR responsibility as it is for the event coordinator to advertise for the upcoming event. YOUR customers should know where to find YOU so they can come out and support you and the other vendors in attendance. Depending on how you sell and produce your products, pickups may be better for your customer than shipping; the offered options may be different at the event versus when an order is placed; perhaps your customer only wants a few items and not an entire minimum order that day. Your job is to make your product availability to your customer as easy as possible and have a successful event. When you do well, there's an opportunity to return for a future event which is now another day you get to earn money. When you have events outside of your city/state AND you have customers where you'll be visiting, you can notify them so they may place orders, which then assist in covering your travel expenses.

Some event coordinators use paper flyers to advertise events in addition to the social media platforms. The key here is to know yourself and the best way to communicate with your audience and followers. Paper flyers can be handed out at events that you are attending in advance and handed out as you mention it to current or potential customers that you encounter that may inquire of your future events. Your website's calendar should be your first go-to. Your audience should be able to easily find you and YOUR website is a great tool. Social Media is good, pending that your audience sees your posts in time. Frequent posting is good, just be sure that you include as much information in the caption/body of the post that is also included in the actual digital flyer. Assuming readers will read everything on the flyer will cause you disappointment. Text messaging and sending emails to your list are other effective methods to share your events. There are ways to automate these processes. If you need assistance or training on how this can be done, consult with a Social Media and Branding specialist. I know of a few that you can contact.

## 11. EVENT CHECKLIST

Proper preparation creates success and prevents poor performance! Preparing yourself the night before will minimize stress on event day. Here is a typical list of the items you will need for your event, which you should customize to match your business. A "simple" setup takes less time to set up.

* Banner & Tablecloth (a customized tablecloth with your logo and company name removes the need for a banner)

* Clipboard(s) - for your order forms, Sale and Inventory Tally sheets

* Order forms - To capture sales for the items you didn't bring, but are available to order, (with a minimum of a deposit or full payment for the order)

* Sale & Inventory Tally sheets - to keep track of what you have on hand and the sales made for the day

* Products - when you have multiple versions of the same item, only put out a few at a time

* Change - $20 minimum, include loose change if necessary

* Postcards/business cards to hand out with or without a purchase. Take a picture or create a digital card which allows you to capture the customer's name and phone number for future contact

* Any orders placed in advance for pickup before, during or after the event

* Charger, extension cord & backup power charger* for your gadgets (in case there isn't a plug close to your table) **Be sure to charge your backup power charger before Event day***

* Rolling cart to carry your items and products easily in and out of the venue

* Staging materials (baskets, stands, etc.)

## SALE & INVENTORY TALLY SHEET

**Date of Event:** _____

**Venue & Address:** _____
_____

**Cost of Table:** _____     **Payment Date for Table:** _____

| Loaves | # of Loaves | Price of Loaves | # of Loaves Sold | Total Sales |
|---|---|---|---|---|
| w/Raisins | | | | |
| CranNut | | | | |
| Chocolate Chips | | | | |
| Keto mini | | | | |
| Vegan | | | | |

Event Gross Sales _____
Pre-Order Sales _____

**Travel Expenses:**
Gas: _____
Food: _____
Vendors: _____
Tolls: _____
Parking: _____
Hotel room: _____

Total Expenses _____
**Net Profit** _____

## 12. EVENT DAY: SHOWING UP & SETTING UP - ON TIME, EVERY TIME

It's the host/ coordinator responsibility to notify you in advance of the start and end times of the event in addition to the set-up and tear down time. It's YOUR responsibility to adhere to these times. You should be aware of how long it takes to set up your table. Plan and manage your time accordingly. It is NOT a good look for an event to start, guests are arriving, looking to purchase and here you are still setting up your table. Yes, some may be willing to wait, most will not, nor is it a guarantee that they'll return once you've set up everything. This also means that you've now allowed money to walk out the door, literally. Some coordinators have now started penalizing for lateness, including turning you away and not refunding your fee. READ your contract, but most importantly, BE ON TIME. If you're running late because of an accident while you're in route, contact the host so they'll know and can make the necessary adjustments. Communication goes a long way.

A BIG complaint I've heard over the years, especially from coordinators that host multiple events a year, are the "No Shows." This occurs more frequently with Direct Sales companies. They will contact the coordinator, pay the fee, sign the contract and the day of the event Not Show Up, nor will they make contact to inform the coordinator of their schedule change, which is VERY inconsiderate. Tables are usually set up in advance and assigned to each vendor. When you fail to show up, there's an empty table with YOUR name and business name on display. With no products to be purchased, no information to be distributed, no money to be made and that's if the host hasn't removed the table altogether. That's a table someone else should've benefited from and money you've just wasted as a business. This also puts you in a position to not be invited to future events. It takes just a few moments to send an email, Private Message, Direct message or even a text to say you will not make it. Your integrity, or lack thereof, is now being shown. Take the time to keep your name in good standing. Remember, people talk and you "Never know who knows whom, that knows YOU."

## 13. INSIDE VS OUTSIDE EVENTS

My very first vending experience came with my first speaking engagement. After being strongly encouraged and informed that being an author also came with speaking engagements, something I did NOT initially want to do. After hearing and processing this new information, I prayed and concluded that: "If God trusts me to do this, then HE will guide me in the process." Within 48 hours of accepting this new task, I received my first request to speak at a church, where a good friend and former co-worker was a over a youth group. She asked that I speak to the group about being an Author and an entrepreneur of multiple businesses. I was also told that I would be able to sell my loaves after the event was over. My setup was simple, especially since I didn't have many options at that time. This same friend later invited me to be a vendor for a larger event that was held in Elyria, OH. Here I was able to meet other small business owners and vendors, where I would begin to learn how Networking works.

My first outside vending experience:

I was encouraged to start vending in 2013 after meeting with a Business Coach, one that I met at the event in Elyria, to expose my Glory Loaves to more people. Up until this time, most of my sales and orders came from friends, family, church members and a few events, which was great for "part-time." Now that I'm doing this full-time the word needed to get out and the sales needed to increase. Though he encouraged me to do this, he did not give me a lot of guidance or instruction on how to make the most of the experience, outside of saying that I need to connect with the customers. The event opportunity was at the Hartville Flea Market located in Hartville, Ohio which is a suburb of Canton. This is a little over an hour from my house and I believe the cost of the table space was about $50. The Organizer in me knew enough to make my area look as welcoming as possible. After speaking with a friend ,who was also a baker, I provided a few samples and "gift packages" since Father's Day was approaching. I did not know much of what to expect from attending, only praying that I will earn enough to make back at least my table fee and gas money from the trip. I'm glad that I had enough foresight to visit this venue in advance of booking a table. I was VERY grateful that I arrived early enough to be placed under the awning along the entrance where customers would pass my table coming AND going. For me, the gift packages were helpful, yet I do not frequently include this at my table now that I have more options for customers to choose from. I've also chosen to not provide samples at regular events because I've learned that 1) the aroma from the loaves naturally draws people over and 2) it would take up extra space and time that I can use for other items. If I'm introducing a new option and I'm looking for feedback, I'll do a tasting, at which time I'm also taking Pre-Orders.

I've done several other outside events over the years, both with my loaves and books and concluded that they are NOT for me. It wasn't so much that they were not successful, but there were things I had to be mindful of:

Though my loaves are packaged, when they are exposed to excessive heat, they can dry out. If you have tasted my loaves, their moistness is part of their signature and we will NOT mess with that. One of the last outside events I did, I had purchased a tent. It turns out that because the setup for us that day was on an asphalt parking lot and I didn't have any way to properly secure the tent. A gust of wind came through twice and destroyed the tent. I was not able to return it to the store because of their policy and the cost to ship it back to the manufacturer, would be more than the cost of the item itself. I accepted the loss and decided this was not meant for me to do. A more recent outside event I found myself participating in, I "assumed" the event would be inside. I was informed by a fellow vendor 2 days before the event that it would be outside. I was leery, but because I had already begun to advertise, I felt it was too late to cancel. It was stated that tents would be provided, so I figured everything would be good. Halfway through the event, the sky opened and POURED down rain!! I got drenched, along with my tablecloth and my display items. I packed up my items as quickly as possible. Once the rain stopped, I spoke with the event coordinator, informed her that I was done for the day and went home. At this point, the odds of me accepting any future outside events are VERY slim.

**Outside vending works better for these types of businesses:**

Clothing/T-shirts

Jewelry/Accessories (sunglasses, purses)

Artwork

Arts & crafts

Books

Health and Financial services

For items like Baked good, Candles, Makeup, Bath & body products (soaps, bath balms, shea butters) be mindful of the temperatures so your product does not melt. This would also be a good thing to advise your customers, if they aren't already aware. Some items may not return to a usable form when they harden after melting.

If you have baked goods or other perishable food products, be mindful and aware of food safety protocols. Have a method to keep applicable items cold or hot. When utensils are used to cut and serve, have a way to keep them rinsed and clean: one bucket with soap & hot water and one to rinse. Food inspectors are subject to appear at any time, so have your bases covered. Certificates, permits and licenses should be obtained prior to the event day and made available when requested. Some cities and counties may have slightly different rules and regulations. Be sure to do your homework prior to accepting the event so that you minimize the risk of being asked to shut your station down and leave the premises, without a refund. The Department of Agriculture is the best place to start for your state's rules and certifications applicable for your business.

## 14. RETURNING CALLS AND MAKING CONNECTIONS

You attend the event, meet the people, collect business cards and flyers - NOW WHAT? Do you add them to a stack of other cards that you'll never contact, or do you organize them for later reference and use? For myself, I've created a system that allows me to keep the cards organized from each event that I can reference later. Emails get added to my list, we connect on Social Media platforms and I'll also put their numbers in my phone. If we've discussed collaborating in the future, I make a note to follow up for a call or meeting. If I enjoyed their product, I will give them a shout out on Social Media when possible. I've also shared future event information with them or passed their information along to someone inquiring. It leaves a bad taste in my mouth if I meet someone, we plan to meet, and the meeting doesn't happen AT ALL! I understand things come up, but let's be considerate of others time as well.

One of the biggest complaints I hear from customers is

failure to return calls, texts and emails from businesses. What can also be considered as "bad business" is for your new customers to not be able to contact you. Every customer you meet is not always "tech savvy," be mindful of this. You are marketing yourself as a business now, this means that your Social Media pages are open to receiving new followers that will see your information and promotions leading to sales. A customer should also be able to call you with questions. If you are reluctant to give out your personal cell number, then create a Google Voice number or have a separate phone for business, whichever is easier for you. This may be the difference in having a repeat customer or losing a sale. The advantage of being a smaller business is the ability to reach and respond to your customers quickly and create a more personal experience. Yes, you should have business hours to adhere to and also respond to inquiries in a timely manner - usually 24-48 business hours. If you cannot commit to a request, be honest about it. Saying "no" is much better than not showing up and all, especially without calling to reschedule or cancel in a timely manner.

Always give your customers great service in addition to reasonable and realistic turnaround times for your products or services. The satisfaction of knowing and feeling that they made a good decision by choosing to conduct business with you will go a LONG way. When they are happy, they will spread the word, which will create new and additional business for you.

## 15. GET YOUR MONEY!

You are a business, in business to make money. You sign up to attend an event as a vendor, Why - To make money. It is YOUR responsibility to ensure your customer will pay you as easily and as efficiently as possible. In today's digital age there are MANY apps that are available to give and receive money. Find, Learn and Use them as quickly as possible. Most of these apps charge a processing fee of some sort. It's the cost of doing business so stop trying to avoid it. Be aware of these fees and use what's best for your business long term.

Here's a short list:

**Cash App** - this has become VERY popular and common in a VERY short time. It's very user-friendly for almost any age. Most of your customers will ask you about this one. You have several options on how quickly you'll receive your money: instantly after each transaction directly into your bank account; you can hold the money on the app and Cash Out when and how much you want to your bank account and there's a Debit Card that loads so you can use it for your business expenses.

**Username:**

_____

**Password:**

_____

**Email:**

_____

**Cash App name:**

$_____


**Square Register/Square Up** - this app allows you to accept credit cards using a device, you can also input the card info manually, send invoices, emails, create eGift cards and sync to create your website if you do not already have one. They also provide Monthly Sales Reports for your records. Your transactions from each business day are automatically processed and deposited into your account the next business day. They now also have an "Instant Deposit" feature that allows you to receive your money the same day if you'd like. This is a good feature to use over a long weekend when you may need your money BEFORE the next business day. (There is an extra fee for this, but it's good to have it, if needed)

**Username:**

_____

**Password:**

_____

**Email:**

_____


**PayPal** - allows you to Send and Receive money with your email address. Many event coordinators use this to collect vendor fees. This creates a safe space in case you need to request a refund, if possible although most table fees are non-refundable and usually stated on the contract. They also have a card processing system, invoicing, instant deposit feature and Debit Card option.


**Username:**

_____

**Password:**

_____

**Email:**

_____

**PayPal Code:**

_____

**PayPal.Me:**

_____


**Venmo** - this is a PayPal service that works like Cash App, only you have to initiate the transfer of funds, which can take 1-3 days, unless you choose Instant Deposit (for a 1% fee, max $10). It's user-friendly and allows you to use emojis to communicate. You can also use this app to make purchases, with or without a Debit Card.

**Username:**

_____

**Password:**

_____

**Email:**

_____

**Venmo name:**

@_____


**Zelle** - banks are starting to offer this feature more now and are usually connected to personal checking and savings accounts. You can receive money into these accounts but cannot send money as business account. As of September 2019, there are no fees to use this feature, but that may change in the future.

Username:

_____

Password:

_____

Email:

_____

CONGRATULATIONS!! You have now completed The Guide for Vendors!! Now you have the knowledge, tips and tools to be successful in your future vending experiences. Reference this guide as often as needed, that's what it is designed for!

We'd love to hear from you! Share your success stories or schedule a consultation to answer your questions on our website: www.areyousurethatyouareready.com Enter/Mention code: AYSTYAR101 to receive $20 off your first session.

**NOTES**

## Notes

*Notes*

## Notes

# ACKNOWLEDGMENTS

Photography by: Raw Glass Photography

Cover Design by: True Creatives Media